A
PUMPKIN
TALE

Sarah and Jacob stood by the window, watching. They could hardly wait for Daddy to get home from work. Today was the day he had promised to help them make a jack-o-lantern. At 5:30 on the dot, Daddy's car pulled into the driveway. "Are you guys ready to go pick out a pumpkin?" he called.

"Hooray!" yelled Jacob.

"Let's go!" cried Sarah, running out to the car.

In a few minutes they arrived at the biggest pumpkin patch the children had ever seen. There were hundreds and hundreds of

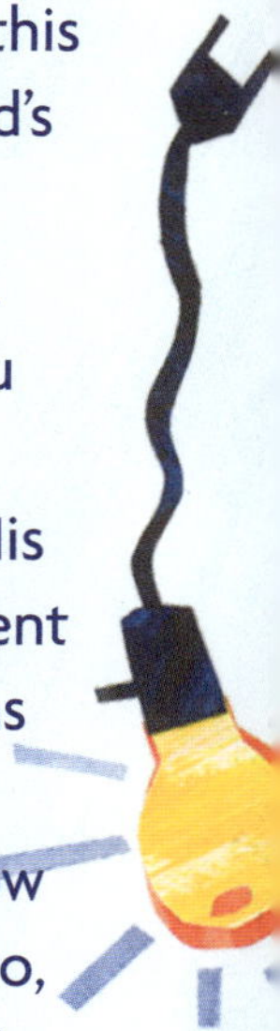

"Ohhh." Sarah thought about this for a moment. "Daddy, I want God's light to shine in my heart."

"Me, too. Me, too," said Jacob.

"I'm glad," Daddy replied. "You know, the Bible says that our sin separates us from God. It keeps His light from shining in us. So God sent His Son Jesus to take away our sins by dying on the cross. Three days later, He rose to life again, and now He lives in heaven. If we ask Him to, He will come and live in our hearts. Then His light will shine in us."

"Let's ask Him right now," said Sarah.

he said, "Do you know that being a Christian is a lot like being a pumpkin?"

"It is?" asked Sarah.

Jacob looked puzzled. "What do you mean?"

"Well," said Daddy, "first God picks each one of us out of the patch. He chooses us to be His very own. Next, He cleans us from the inside out. He scoops all the yucky stuff out of our hearts—the sin—the bad things we say or do. After that, He puts a great big smile on our faces. His light shines in our hearts. Then everyone can see His love in us!"

pumpkins. Big ones, small ones. Round ones, long ones. Yellow and orange and green. Sarah and Jacob walked up and down every row, searching for just the right pumpkin for their jack-o-lantern. "There—look at that one!" Sarah pointed. It was the roundest, largest, brightest orange pumpkin in the patch. Jacob could hardly get his arms around it.

"I think you found the perfect pumpkin," Daddy smiled. They carried it back to the car. When they got home, Daddy placed the pumpkin on the kitchen table. As he began to carve the jack-o-lantern,

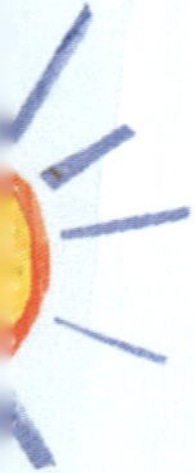

Would you like Jesus to live in your heart? Would you like God's light to shine in you? Just pray,

"Dear God, I'm sorry for the bad things I've done. Thank You for sending Jesus to take away my sins. Please come into my heart and fill my life with Your light. Help others to see Your love in me. Amen."

Christin Ditchfield

CROSSWAY

GOOD NEWS *Tracts*

www.goodnewstracts.org

ISBN 978-1-6821-6194-4

50299